The message of this book is vital for the protectio⌐ ⌐⌐⌐⌐ ⌐⌐⌐
preservation of our families, our churches, and ⌐⌐⌐ ⌐⌐⌐ ⌐⌐⌐
It is a must read!   This book has th⌐ ⌐⌐⌐
and loosing that Jesus gave Peter ⌐⌐⌐
wants to destroy and loosing Go⌐
Apostle Mike has provided in simple ter                     all who
are desiring to know how to pray                     ⌐ crisis.

### APOSTLE EMANUELE CANNISTRACI
*Prophet, Teacher, Evangelist, Missionary*


Every Christian needs to read this book for the purpose of
understanding and practicing the principles presented.
The truth and practice of praying hedges, God's protection
around all we do and have, authorizes God to send His holy
angels to supernaturally preserve and protect us.
These prayers are not prayed from fear and worry but
from biblical knowledge, faith, and confidence.
Thanks, Apostle Servello, for sharing with the Body of Christ
these vital truths that you have proven to be workable realities.

### DR. BILL HAMON
*Bishop/Apostle, Christian International Ministries*
*Author of* Day of the Saints *and many other books*


I am very excited about Apostle Mike Servello's new book.
I have known Mike for a number of years and I
have seen the work that God is doing through his life and
ministry. I do not hesitate to recommend this new work that he
presents to the body of Christ. It will bless your life!

### HAROLD CABALLEROS
*Pastor of El Shaddai Church in Guatemala*

*Dedicated to the wonderful family God has given me.*

*To my Aunt Angie who went to be with the Lord while I was completing this book.*

*To Aunt Mary who stills believes I can do no wrong and that this will be*

*the best selling book ever written besides the Bible!*

*To my Mom and Dad who have always encouraged me.*

*To my wife, Barbara, who has always believed in me and supported me.*

*To my son, Michael, and his wife, Melissa, my son, Joey, and his wife Kelly.*

*To my little buddy, Matthew, my first grandchild, and to my daughter, Rachel.*

*To the Mt. Zion church family whom I have loved and pastored for over 20 years.*

*To my faithful intercessors and staff - you have always been a source*

*of strength and a shield of protection -*

*you guys are the best!*

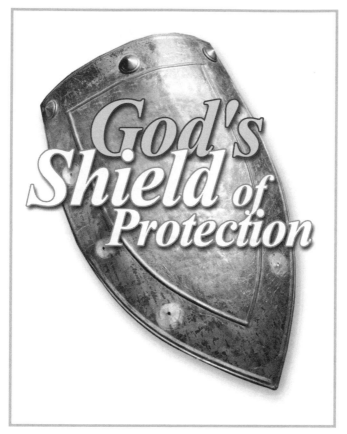

# PASTOR MIKE SERVELLO

*Mt* Zion Ministries

## ⁓Mt Zion Ministries
931 Herkimer Road
Utica, New York 13502
*315.792.4748 • www.mzm.org*

Mt Zion Ministries is a local church with a vision to reach the world. We are a non-denominational Christian church that believes the Bible is the Word of God. We are here to teach people how to live a better life by getting help from the One who gave us life.

Published by *Lifes*Truth *a division of*
DS*Lisi* Inc.
8271 Rt 274, PO Box 171, Holland Patent, NY 13354 • www.lifestruth.com

Editing: Beth Clark, Jim Donnelly, Mike Hughes,
Marianne Lange, Kim Lisi and Paula Quick
Cover and Interior Design: Stephen Lisi

# CONTENTS

# PREFACE

We are living in very peculiar times. Not only are they changing times, but violent times. The world was shaken when many watched on September 11, 2001 as two landmark buildings, the Twin Towers of the World Trade Center, fell. Not only were we shocked, but also we were confused because of the emotional trauma that entered into the very hearts and depths of our soul. Then, the unknown which always produces fear, began to cause many to wonder what lies ahead. In the middle of these types of emotions and confused times, there comes a message that helps each one of us grab hold of God's grace and blessings and begin to pray again with faith. God's Protective Hedge is that message. Pastor Mike Servello has penned a message that gives us practical steps, ignites our faith, and teaches us how to pray in peculiar times.

God's Protective Hedge - what a wonderful grouping of words. Of course, even when I saw the title I thought of the first place "hedge" is used in the Bible. This is where Satan enters into the presence of God and begins to remind Him of His protection around Job. He converses with God to say that, "You've built this boundary around Job's life, his house, and everything he has. Because of this, You have blessed the work of his hands and You've increased the substance in his hands" (Paraphrased Job 1:10). It is as if the Devil is saying, "The only way I can get to Job is for You to remove the protection You have around him. If You just move this protection, I will ravish everything Job has because I can't destroy what Job has as long as You are protecting it." Every time I read this verse, I feel great peace flood my spirit. This reminds me, as God's children, we are protected as long as we remain in the abiding place with Him.

My family was very much like Job. God had blessed the work of my Dad's hands. We lived on a beautiful acreage, in a beautiful home, with wonderful substance. All of this was fenced in and had hedges of protection. This was an incredibly beautiful place; however, there came a time that the hedges seemed to be broken down. The enemy flooded to overtake all of what was there plus the future blessings that God had intended. The enemy had found weakened places, or gaps, and entered in to bring destruction. When I was 18, the Lord spoke to me and told me He could restore all that I had lost and rebuild the ruins, and re-establish the hedges. Most of us have experienced situations as I have described above. Even though we know God has great blessings, we have watched many of those blessings slip away. I have gone through a 30 year learning process of seeking the Lord and watching Him rebuild and watching Him build a hedge around my life and secure the blessings that were in the generations of my bloodline. God has used Pastor Mike Servello to put in words what I know is right and what I have labored to see happen. What is so incredible about this book is that Pastor Mike shows us how to co-labor with God to build or rebuild that protection that we need to go into our future.

A hedge is a boundary formed by a dense row of unusually thorny shrubs. In the Bible, hedges served to protect vineyards from damage by animals or intruders. To hedge means to hem in, set an obstruction for your enemies and to protect. In Biblical times, when a vineyard was being prepared, part of that preparation was to terrace the hillsides and clear the ground of stones. These stones when piled high would become a protective hedge. These walls or hedges protected the grapes that would produce the new wine. One danger was for little foxes to break through the wall and overtake the vines, crushing the grapes, and actually destroying the vines. Sometimes, the hedge of thorns was actually planted on top of the wall of stone. Pastor Servello shows us how to put up hedges in a way that we can protect ourselves from not only destruction but also even the little foxes.

I have known Pastors Mike and Barbara and have watched them build hedges in every area of their lives. Because they have built them, they now have a blueprint to help others. Because their faith has been tested and tried, and they have walked in integrity and wholeness in ministry, they can impart to us a true testimony that can help each one of us who reads this book build for the future. As you read God's Protective Hedge, just feel a new rebuilding process occurring in your spirit and feel God's protective covering surrounding your boundaries. This is a season in the Body of Christ with a need for protection. This is also a season that God is producing fruit on the vine that will be the revelation that is needed for us to advance in His Kingdom purposes in the earth. As you read and pray this protective hedge, also receive the revelation you need to enter the future with boldness.

CHUCK D. PIERCE

*Vice President, Global Harvest Ministries*
*President, Glory of Zion International Ministries, Inc.*

# FOREWORD

Mike Servello is one of the practitioners in the body of Christ who can apply truth in a specific manner that produces measurable results. He has applied the truths of financial freedom, serving your community, power evangelism and building a strong local church to his geographic area and has affected the political realm, the educational realm, the spiritual realm and the financial realm.

Mike is truly a forerunner to what many pastors, churches and ministries should be doing. His church is seeing the treasures of God opened up and resources poured into their hands to be used for the furtherance of the kingdom of God. Mike is not only a proven pastor, teacher, great family man and great friend, he is also a man of integrity with an impeccable reputation and an example to his city and the nation.

I recommend this book very highly. It is more than simply a textbook; it is a product of his life and ministry and an example for us to follow.

**FRANK DAMAZIO**
*Senior Pastor, City Bible Church, Portland, Oregon*

# Introduction

*"The secret things belong to the Lord our God, but those things which are revealed belong to us and our children forever"* (Deuteronomy 29:29).

Aren't you glad that the Lord chooses to reveal certain things to us? I am. The principles in this book are prayer strategies I have come to understand by the revelation of the Holy Spirit over the course of several years. During a time when "wars and rumors of wars" abound around the world, I believe these things will help you pray effectively for protection in many areas of your life.

My intention is not to give a never-fail formula for prayer or to attempt to put God in a box, because to do so would fly in the face of our God who knows all, sees all and is forever in control of everything that happens on earth. The strategies, however, I will share in the following pages have come from years of seeking the Lord's counsel concerning effective prayer.

Everything in this book has been tried and true in my own life as I have prayed for the protection of my family, my work, my possessions and myself. I believe every one of these principles to be true and effective, but I would like to tell you a story of something that happened to us, even in the midst of faithful, diligent prayer.

Our family once included a very special lady who was like a second mom to me and like a grandmother to my children. During the summer of 2002, she and my son were driving home when a reckless driver hit them head-on. The young man who hit them was racing with a friend and tried to pass two cars when he slammed into my son and aunt.

My son was driving, and the impact was on his side of the car. The car was completely destroyed while my son sustained only minor injuries. My aunt was injured very seriously and passed away after three weeks in intensive care.

As you can imagine, I began to ask the big question, "*Why God?*" The Lord simply spoke to my heart and told me to trust Him and His wisdom. The scripture He gave me was *Daniel 3:21*, which tells the story of three young Hebrew men who were suddenly taken from their normal lives. They were in their everyday clothes, which indicates that they had no time to prepare and were tied up and thrown into a fiery furnace.

*Daniel 3:21-27*

*21 So these men, wearing their robes, trousers, turbans and other clothes, were bound and thrown into the blazing furnace.*

*22 The king's command was so urgent and the furnace so hot that the flames of the fire killed the soldiers who took up Shadrach, Meshach and Abednego, 23 and these three men, firmly tied, fell into the blazing furnace.*

*24 Then King Nebuchadnezzar leaped to his feet in amazement and asked his advisers, "Weren't there three men that we tied up and threw into the fire?" They replied, "Certainly, O king."*

*25 He said, "Look! I see four men walking around in the fire, unbound and unharmed, and the fourth looks like a son of the gods."*

*26 Nebuchadnezzar then approached the opening of the blazing furnace and shouted, "Shadrach, Meshach and Abednego, servants of the Most High God, come out! Come here!" So Shadrach, Meshach and Abednego came out of the fire, 27 and the satraps, prefects, governors and royal advisers crowded around them. They saw that the fire had not harmed their bodies, nor was a hair of their heads singed; their robes were not scorched, and there was no smell of fire on them (NIV).*

Trials come upon us suddenly and unexpectedly often giving us no time to prepare. Just like the young men in Daniel, no one likes to be tied up, bound or restricted in any way. This sudden attack led these young men to an experience of finding the Lord in the midst of their fiery trial. Perhaps you know the story. They emerged unbound and unburned from the blazing furnace; they didn't even smell like smoke, and they had a fresh revelation of God.

Two days into my aunt's hospitalization, doctors delivered a shocking piece of news - she had a very advanced form of lung cancer. She had no idea that she even had cancer. During our difficult three-week journey while she was in intensive care, I saw the Lord's incredible faithfulness to us every step of the way. Although she died from the injuries sustained in the car crash, I believe she was spared much suffering and anguish that would have come from dealing with her illness.

The entire experience did not shake our family's faith but deepened it. The Lord used it to encourage many people in our congregation. They conveyed that they had drawn strength from my preaching through the years, yet had never been so strengthened as when they observed the way my family and I walked through this trying time.

I share this story to affirm the wisdom and sovereignty of God in every situation. He calls us to pray in every circumstance. The purpose of this book is to present and define some prayer principles that I have found to be extremely sound and effective in my own life and in the lives of others. They are prayer tactics, in the spirit of *Deuteronomy 29:29*, which have been revealed by the Lord and proven to be a great blessing; I pray they will be a blessing in your life as well.

**Deuteronomy 29:29** *The secret things belong to the LORD our God, but the things revealed belong to us and to our children forever, that we may follow all the words of this law (NIV).*

# Praying Protective Hedges

## Chapter One

Many times, messages are birthed in the difficult places of our lives. That is exactly where the principles you will read about in this book were burned into my heart.

The year was 1995, and I was threatened by someone who was determined to destroy me personally and to devastate the church I pastor. Just prior to that, the Lord had led me to confront sin in another ministry. Now, I know how serious the confrontation of sin is, but let me reiterate that I took that action after much prayer as a step of obedience to the Lord.

The threats against the church and me came as a direct response to the confronting of sin. The man who threatened me came to our city specifically to establish a ministry to destroy ours!

I immediately went into a time of prayer and began to seek God's heart and strategy concerning how I needed to handle that situation and deal with that person. What He spoke to my heart shocked me. The Lord gave me two instructions. First, He said not to speak a word against the person who was threatening us. Secondly, He said to pray a "hedge of protection" around myself, my family and our church.

I tried to recall a biblical example of a protective hedge and remembered the story of Job (*Job 1:9, 10*). Every day I began to pray, "Lord, place a hedge of protection around us as You did around Job. You told me to pray this way, so I believe that you are shielding and keeping us safe behind Your protective hedge..." As I continued to pray in this manner, the Lord revealed more and more to me about building protective hedges.

*Job 1:9 So Satan answered the LORD and said, "Does Job fear God for nothing?*
*10 Have You not made a hedge around him, around his household, and around all that he has on every side? You have blessed the work of his hands, and his possessions have increased in the land.*

After six months, I received word that the person who had come against us had moved out of our city in disgrace. I did not rejoice in this person's failure. The entire incident did cause me to see just how much power exists in praying protective hedges around the people and things for which God has given us affection and responsibility.

The situation also inspired me to incorporate praying a hedge of protection around my life. In the months and years that followed, the Lord led me to pray different kinds of protective hedges around myself, my family and our church as we found ourselves engaged in various battles. For more than three years, I did not feel the Lord's release to share with anyone about the kind of praying I had been doing or about what He had taught me about praying protective hedges.

In January 1999 I knew it was finally time to speak to our congregation concerning the prayer lessons I had been learning. I shared the entire journey with them and began to teach them how to pray protective hedges as well. Their response was overwhelming. As they began to pray in the same manner, we saw faith increase in people's lives and more victory in daily battles.

Since then, I have shared these insights in many different settings with a variety of audiences around the world. The response is always the same -

lives change as people begin to integrate these principles into their prayer times.

At the dawn of the twenty-first century, the world is filled with tragedy and devastation. We desperately need the Lord's protection. Newspapers, magazines and television broadcasts offer less and less good news, while reporting more and more stories that are shocking, unsettling and sometimes too horrible to believe. Indeed, the darkness is increasing. Consequently, we must guard our hearts against fear in this evil hour and learn to be pro-active in prayer concerning our lives, our families, our homes, our nations and everything else God has given us.

As we think about praying for protection in various areas of our lives, it is important to understand that prayer is not a cause-and-effect formula, and that the presence of sin in our lives can hinder our prayers.

Our lives need to be aligned with the truth of God's Word in order for these prayer tactics to be effective. For instance, I will write about praying a hedge of protection around our minds. We can pray a mental hedge all day long, but it will not keep us protected the way God intends if we allow ungodly images to enter our minds through ungodly movies, exposure to violence or filthy language.

Similarly, praying a hedge of protection against disease or infirmity will be counteracted by

eating nothing but junk food or by refusing to exercise and take care of ourselves. As we go forward, let's
assume that our prayers will be accompanied by wise
choices and diligence to live our lives according to
God's Word by the power of His Spirit.

When I look at the discouraging landscape of
our world, one of the passages that most strengthens
my heart is *Psalm 91*. Perhaps you know this passage
well, or maybe you have never read it. Regardless of
your familiarity with these words, I want you to have
a fresh encounter with this powerful portion of God's
Word:

> *Live under the protection*
> *of God Most High and stay in*
> *the shadow of God All-Powerful.*
> *Then you will say to the LORD,*
> *"You are my fortress, my place of safety;*
> *you are my God, and I trust you."*
> *The Lord will keep you safe*
> *from secret traps and deadly diseases.*
> *He will spread his wings over you*
> *and keep you secure. His faithfulness*
> *is like a shield or a city wall.*
> *You won't need to worry about*
> *dangers at night or arrows during*
> *the day. And you won't fear diseases*
> *that strike in the dark or sudden*

*disaster at noon.*

*You will not be harmed, though
thousands fall all around you.*

*And with your own eyes you
will see the punishment of the wicked.*

*The LORD Most High is your
fortress. Run to him for safety,
and no terrible disasters will strike
you or your home.*

*God will command his angels
to protect you wherever you go.*

*They will carry you in their
arms, and you won't hurt your
feet on the stones.*

*You will overpower the strongest
lions and the most deadly snakes.*

*The Lord says, "If you love me
and truly know who I am, I will
rescue you and keep you safe.*

*When you are in trouble,
call out to me. I will answer and
be there to protect and honor you.*

*You will live a long life and
see my saving power."*

*Psalm 91 (CEV)*

# Living In God's Secret Place

## Chapter Two

"He who dwells in the secret place of the Most High, shall abide under the shadow of the Almighty" (Psalm 91:1).

There really is a "secret place" in God; He has a place where we can dwell in safety. Decide right now that you are going to dwell in the secret place. Refuse to be afraid regardless of what happens in your life or in the world. Determine to stay at peace, which is evidence that the Spirit of God lives in you.

> **Galatians 5: 22** *But the fruit of the Spirit is love, joy, peace, patience, kindness, goodness, faithfulness, 23 gentleness and self-control. Against such things there is no law. (KJV).*

You can live in peace when you know that you are in the secret place. I have found in God's Word that He has some "secret places" for His people. Biblically, to be in the "secret place" means to be sheltered, hidden and concealed from your enemies. It is a place of refuge! The Bible refers to secret places God has for us, and I would like to share three of them.

## The House of God

The Lord wants us to find refuge and protection in His house. There is an instinctive drive in people that causes them to seek God during times of trouble. Somehow, I believe, they know that there is a place of safety in the Lord, and there is.

*Psalm 27:5* says, *"For in the time of trouble He shall hide me in His pavilion; in the secret place of His tabernacle He shall hide me."* The house of God is much more than the building where a church meets. It is the family of God, those who believe in Him. There is safety in the fellowship that exists and in the power of unity among believers.

Who can forget the events of September 11, 2001? Our nation was in a state of panic, and basically everything was shut down - airports, malls, schools and businesses; yet, there was one place that remained open - churches!

People were supernaturally drawn to the house of God and filled churches across the land. We are instinctively drawn to God's house in times of trouble. Something inside of us knows there is a place of safety in Him, and in that place His presence dwells.

## The Presence of God

*Psalm 31:19, 20* says, *"Oh, how great is Your goodness, which You have laid up for those who fear You, which You have prepared for those who trust in You in the presence of the sons of men! You shall hide them in the secret place of Your presence from the plots of man..."*

Would the devil want to be in God's presence? Of course not! He hates God, and when we are in God's presence, we are safe. I encourage you to live in God's presence not only in your prayer closet, but everywhere you go, praying silently, worshiping in your heart and acknowledging the presence of the Lord within you by the Spirit all day long and even through the night.

## Prayer and Worship

*Psalm 32:6, 7* tells us, *"For this cause everyone who is godly shall pray to You in a time when You may be found; surely in a flood of great waters they*

*shall not come near him. You are my hiding place;*
*You shall preserve me from trouble; You shall sur-*
*round me with songs of deliverance. Selah"*

Just as the devil hates God's presence, he also
hates prayer and worship. The spiritual power in
prayer and worship will cause him to flee as you draw
near to God. We must pray and worship often and
rest in the security that exists therein.

The house of God, the presence of God, and
prayer and worship - these are some of the Lord's
"secret places" of refuge. They are places we need to
stay in order for our prayers to be most effective.
They are strong towers that resist the enemy.

# Satan Spills the Beans

*Chapter Three*

Sometimes we have to back up before we can go forward. Go to the book of Job before we look again at *Psalm 91*. If the books of the Bible were in chronological order, the first book would be Job. The forty-two chapters in this book contain the earliest recorded dealings of God with man. In the beginning of this most ancient book is an intriguing scene I would paraphrase something like this:

One day the sons of God came to present themselves and Satan came also among them. The Lord said to Satan, "Where have you been?"

Satan, who roams about like a lion seeking people to devour, replied, "Well, I've been up and down and all over the place."

> *I Peter 5: 8 - Be sober, be vigilant; because your adversary the devil walks about like a roaring lion, seeking whom he may devour. 9 Resist him, steadfast in the faith, knowing that the same sufferings are experienced by your brotherhood in the world.*

The Lord, knowing that Satan was looking for someone to harass, said, "Have you considered my servant, Job?" That's right. God actually said to the devil, "How about Job? What about him? Have you been around his house?"

Here's the intriguing part. Satan himself said in *Job 1:9, "Does Job fear God for nothing?" ... "Have you not put a hedge around him and his household and everything he has? You have blessed the work of his hands, so that his flocks and herds are spread throughout the land" (NIV).*

Satan is the first one to tell us that God has a protective hedge around us! Isn't that amazing? Our enemy tells us how powerless he is against us! The words come out of his own mouth. He essentially said, "There is a shield around Job. I see it. I was there. I can't touch him."

There are two ways Satan can touch us. One way we break the shield is through sin, unbelief, fear, disobedience, unforgiveness, judgment or some other attitude or action that is contrary to God's Word. The second way is when God gives him permission to come into our territory. Now, if God gives Satan permission to attack you or deal with you, you can be certain that permission has been granted in order to build your faith. As a result you will emerge stronger and better in the end.

When you are under an attack from the enemy, first ask, "Did I open a door?" Look at the attitudes of your heart; examine your motives; rehearse what you have said because "out of the abundance of the heart the mouth speaks."

> *Matthew 12:34 How can you, being evil, speak good things? For out of the abundance of the heart the mouth speaks.*

If you have not sinned, say, "Lord, whatever You want to teach me, I'm a quick learner. I'm all ears! I know that after You've tried me, I will come out of this like gold." Confess *Job 23:10,* which says, *"But He knows the way that I take; when He has tested me, I shall come forth as gold."*

You are not the devil's punching bag. Do you believe that? You are not the devil's kickball. No, you have been given authority over him, and you are to kick him around! He knows it. He's known it since the first chapter of the first book when he admitted, "I can't touch those people!"

Put your own name in the blank and tell yourself, "(Your name), Satan cannot touch me."

Another translation of the Bible renders *Job 1:10* this way, *"You're like a wall protecting not only him but his entire family and all of his property. You make him successful whatever he does and his flocks and his herds are everywhere"* (CEV).

Read again what Satan said to the Lord. *"You're like a wall protecting not only him but his entire family and all of his property. You make him successful whatever he does and his flocks and his herds are everywhere."* We can learn a lesson from the enemy's camp. Satan himself declares that God's protective hedges are established around at least three aspects of your life: you personally, your family and your possessions.

It is possible to have hedges that Satan cannot penetrate; we must understand all that rightly belongs to us in God, by faith, and apprehend it.

# Seven Shields of Protection

## Chapter Four

Looking through the Bible, there are many specific areas of our lives protected by the Lord. I would like to share and explain seven of these hedges of protection, which are shields that Satan cannot penetrate. These shields are in effect all around you, your family and your possessions. I urge you to begin confessing them around your life and all that concerns you. I have practiced this kind of prayer in my life, and others have too. These prayer shields have proven to be effective.

## The Blood of Jesus Christ -
### Shield of Redemption

The most powerful shield of protection around our lives is the blood of Jesus Christ. We are washed in the blood when we become children of God. *Colossians 1:14* says, *"In Him we have redemption through His blood."* *Revelation 1:5* tells us that Jesus *"loved us and washed us from our sins in His own blood."* Notice that the Bible tells us that Jesus loves us first; then He washes us from our sin. This is awesome news! Because we have redemption, we have been bought out of the slavery of sin.

Satan has no claim on us - no right to us. *Ephesians 1:7* says, *"He is so rich in kindness that he purchased our freedom through the blood of his Son, and our sins are forgiven."* (NLT) When we are forgiven, we are right with God. Satan cannot cut through the hedge of protection that surrounds us with the blood of Jesus.

Perhaps the most straightforward verse in the Bible related to overcoming the enemy is *Revelation 12:11, "And they overcame him by the blood of the Lamb and by the word of their testimony..."* Put your name in that verse, "(Your name) overcomes Satan." How? By the blood of the Lamb and the word of your testimony. You are saying to the enemy, "God's got a shield around me, and you are not going to break it!"

Do not allow Satan to believe the Bible more

than you do. You are an overcomer; therefore, live an overcoming life. While he knows he cannot break God's hedge, you must also be convinced that you are completely covered and altogether protected by the hedge of the Lord. Today, you are able to overcome the enemy the same way those believers who are written of in the book of Revelation did - by the blood of the Lamb.

## God the Father -
### Shield of Relationship/Intimacy

Another protective hedge around us is God the Father, *your* Father. When you are washed in the blood of Jesus, God becomes your Father. He becomes your Dad. He's your Papa. You no longer have the spirit of bondage again to fear, but you have the spirit of adoption, which enables you to cry out to the Lord, "Papa! Father!" (*Romans 8:15*).

In *Genesis 15:1* the word of the Lord came to Abram in a vision. Basically, God said, "Don't be afraid, Abram. Do not be afraid. Why? I am your shield. I'm a hedge around you. I am your very great reward."

You may say, "Great, but that was Abram. What about me?" Read *Galatians 3:29* which says, *"If you belong to Christ, then you are Abraham's seed, and heirs according to the promise"* (NIV). Therefore, whatever God promised Abraham also belongs to you if you are in Christ. Because that is true, I often quote *Genesis 15:1* to myself. I think about the Lord saying, "The word of the Lord came to Mike. 'Don't be afraid, Mike. I am your shield, your very great reward.'" Then I pray it back to God, "Lord, You're my shield, You're my very great reward."

> *Genesis 15:1 - After this, the word of the LORD came to Abram in a vision: "Do not be afraid, Abram. I am your shield, your very great reward " (NIV).*

Those words are as living and active for *you* as they are for me. I beg you to take God's Word personally. Do not read it as though you're reading about someone else. It is your life you're reading about! God's Word is for you!

Let's look at two more scriptures starting with *Psalm 3*. In verse 1 David says, *"Lord, how are they increased that trouble me!"* Do you ever have one of those days, when your troubles seem to overwhelm you? David looked around and saw nothing but problems increasing all around him. He continued, *"Many are they that rise up against me. Many there be which say of my soul, There is no help for him in God."* How discouraging! Can you imagine being in such bad shape that people say, "Even God can't help this guy!"?

But look at what comes next: *"Selah."* As David stopped to selah, to pause and reflect on his situation, he realized something awesome and said to the Lord, *"But You, O Lord, are a shield for me; You are my glory and the lifter of my head."* Then everything changed.

David's whole perspective shifted because he understood that God's shield was round about him. He saw that victory was not only possible but secure; he declared, *"Now my head will be lifted up above my enemies because God is protecting me. God is around me."* This is as true for you in your situation as it was for David. God is around you, protecting you - and your victory is secure.

1 John 4:4 states, *"Greater is He that is in you than he that is in the world"* (KJV). We are talking about the One who lives inside us - the mighty, awesome Spirit of the living God. Do not sell yourself short - The Greater One, The Mighty One, The Victorious One, lives inside of you. He is greater than any devil, any demon, any force of darkness that would come against you. No matter what you face, He is greater. He is the overcoming Lord whose purpose in coming to earth was to destroy the works of the enemy.

> **I John 3:8** - *...For this purpose the Son of God was manifested, that He might destroy the works of the devil.*

## The Angels of God -
### Shield of the Resources of Heaven

God's angels form a third type of hedge

around us. God gives His angels to us to protect us. Sometimes I am astounded by the amount of faith people have in demonic power. I often hear them confessing how awful, how powerful, how devastating these attacks against them have been. They say things like, "Well, this demon did this, and that demon did that...." I know demons are real and active, but more importantly, let's consider the angels of God. We must understand that there are more angels for us than demons against us!

God's angels are like a living shield ministering His protection to us. The Bible tells us that angels are sent to minister for us. *Hebrews 1:14* says concerning angels, *"Are they not all ministering spirits sent forth to minister for those who will inherit salvation?"* We are the heirs of salvation; we are the ones to whom the angels are sent. God's people have always been the ones *for* whom and *to* whom angels ministered.

In *Genesis 48:16* Jacob gave credit to one of God's angels when he said, *"...the Angel... who delivered me from all harm -- may he bless these boys, my children..."* (NIV). Additionally, in *Exodus 23:20* the Lord said to Moses, *"See, I am sending an angel ahead of you to guard you along the way and to bring you to the place I have prepared"* (NIV).

One of my favorite stories about angels is in *2 Kings 19*. The wicked king, Sennacherib of Assyria, was like a steamroller. Once he began to move against a city or a nation, no army could stop him. The cities and nations crumbled at his hand. Wherever he went, he conquered, and his conquests increased as did his pride.

When this puffed-up leader came against Jerusalem, in essence he said to King Hezekiah, "Let me tell you something: God sent me, and I am going to destroy you!" Furthermore, he said to the people, "Don't let Hezekiah deceive you. You are defeated. Nobody is going to stop me." He then proceeded to send Hezekiah a letter in which he mocked God and ridiculed Hezekiah. King Hezekiah then took the letter to Isaiah the prophet, who laid it on the altar and began to pray.

I can almost hear the prophet crying out, "Oh God, what do we do?" The word of the Lord came to Isaiah's heart, and he prophesied to Hezekiah that the Lord said, "I'm going to defend this city and save it for my sake. Don't worry about it."

That night, the angel of the Lord moved through the Assyrian camp and put to death 185,000 men. When the people got up the next morning, the ground was covered with dead bodies. This is the power of just one angel!

We do not understand the power of the spiritual realm. Jesus knew what He was talking about when He said, "Right now I could call twelve legions of angels...." If one angel killed 185,000 men in one night, can you imagine what twelve legions of angels could have done to Jerusalem and the armies of Rome?

God promises that His angels are keeping charge over us. *Psalm 34:7* says, *"The angel of the LORD encamps all around those who fear Him, and delivers them."* Do you fear God? The angel of the Lord is camping out wherever we go. We must not fear the devil; we must fear and revere God. We must remember that there are more for us than against us. It does not matter what comes against you.  It does not matter what threatens to kill you, steal from you or destroy your life, because there are more that are *for* you than *against* you.

God's power to bless and keep you is greater than the devil's power to deceive and take from you. Mighty angels are on guard around you - God's angels, angels full of power. They do encamp around you and are moving in your midst, keeping watch over you and your family. According to *Psalm 91:11,* *"God has given His angels charge over you, to keep you in all your ways."*

## The Full Armor of God

The first three hedges mentioned here are shields of protection that God gives us. But this one is something for which we must take personal responsibility. The full armor of God, as mentioned in

*Ephesians* 6, is a powerful shield of protection for us. When Paul begins to deal with the issue of spiritual warfare in this chapter, he says, *"Get fully dressed. Do not go out undressed; put on the full armor of God!"* What soldier would go into battle without his weapons and protective gear? We are engaged in warfare with supernatural powers. We must have supernatural protection.

I can tell when people are not wearing their armor - no helmet of salvation, no Word of God on their mind, no breastplate of righteousness, no buckler of truth, no feet shod with the preparation of the gospel of peace, no shield of faith, and no sword of the spirit. They're undressed. When people are undressed, they are vulnerable - easy prey for the enemy. The Bible says that when we "get dressed," we are able to stand against every onslaught of the powers of hell.

When you put on your armor and go to war, the devil cannot get you. When he throws things at you, they bounce right off your helmet or your shield and fall to the ground. You also have your sword. You're covered with armor, and armor protects you. There is a spiritual war raging, and when we walk onto the battlefield (which is all around us) without our armor on, is it any wonder that we end up bruised and bleeding?

As we go through the Christian life, we continually find ourselves engaged in spiritual conflict - the unseen war in the supernatural realm. Some people are easy targets due to prayerlessness, lack of faith or any number of other reasons. Some are easy targets simply because they are not covered in the armor of God. When we are clothed in God's armor, things that could destroy others will not destroy us. We must put on our armor; we must wear the protective clothing of the Lord if we are going to be serious about living victorious lives and advancing God's kingdom.

Once we have put on our armor, then we stand. We do not run from the battle; we stand firmly upon the confidence that God's armor is effective - it covers us and protects us from the fiery darts of the enemy. When it's all over, we go forward in the name of Jesus.

*Ephesians 6 : 11 - Put on the full armor of God so that you can take your stand against the devil's schemes. 12 For our struggle is not against flesh and blood, but against the rulers, against the authorities, against the powers of this dark world and against the spiritual forces of evil in the heavenly realms. 13 Therefore put on the full armor of God, so that when the day of evil comes, you may be able to stand your ground, and after you have done everything, to stand. 14 Stand firm then, with the belt of truth buckled around your waist, with the breastplate of righteousness in place, 15 and with your feet fitted with the readiness that comes from the gospel of peace. 16 In addition to all this, take up the shield of faith, with which you can extinguish all the flaming arrows of the evil one. 17 Take the helmet of salvation and the sword of the Spirit, which is the word of God (NIV).*

## Faith

Faith builds a hedge. We have to believe.
*I John 5:4* reminds us, *"This is the victory that has overcome the world - our faith."* Our faith overcomes the world. One of our most powerful weapons is faith!

We can have all the truth there is, but if we do not believe, the truth within us is dry and powerless. When we deal with spiritual warfare and demonic powers, we must believe. We have to believe that we have authority and exercise that authority in the supernatural realm.

Let me give you an example that comes from more than twenty years of experience.

There are times when the enemy will try to invade my home with strife or fear, or to launch an all-out assault against one of my children. When that happens, I immediately begin to confront him at the invasion point and push him back. I declare, "You are not coming in here! You must go out the same way you came in! I will war against you as long as it takes for you to retreat in defeat!"

How can I take on the enemy that way? Because I know my authority as a believer (*Luke 10:19; 1 John 4:4*), and I exercise it through faith. I believe in it enough to impose it on the hosts of hell. Do you know what? They turn around and run (*James 4:7*)!

*Luke 10:19 - Behold, I give you the authority to trample on serpents and scorpions, and over all the power of the enemy, and nothing shall by any means hurt you.*

*I John 4:4 - You, dear children, are from God and have overcome them, because the one who is in you is greater than the one who is in the world (NIV).*

*James 4:7 - Submit yourselves therefore to God. Resist the devil, and he will flee from you (KJV).*

This is how we live - and how we must live - as God's people. There is a measure of faith you must have just to keep your own life in order. Then you go a little higher, and you need a little more to keep your family in order. As we grow and our spheres of influence widen, our faith increases and we are more and more able to exercise the authority that belongs to us in Jesus.

Remember the shield of faith? *Ephesians 6:16* states, *"In every battle you will need faith as your shield to stop the fiery arrows aimed at you by Satan" (TLB).* Some scholars believe that those "fiery arrows" refer to demonic spirits. I, too, believe those arrows are demonic spirits, but I also know the Bible says that faith stops the onslaught of the powers of darkness, and faith keeps us protected.

## Integrity

One of the character qualities that will build a protective hedge around you is integrity. I like to define integrity as, "honesty, soundness, completeness and wholeness." A person with integrity is a whole person, one who has an undivided heart and who is committed to walk righteously before the Lord.

Sin puts a big target on you, a bull's eye for the devil. You can be fully dressed in your armor, and through lack of integrity, have a big target in one particular area of your life. It's like a billboard saying, "Hey, devil, shoot me right here because this is where I'm vulnerable."

Sin will destroy your life *(Romans 6:23)*. When you deal with sin properly and ask the Lord to forgive and cleanse you, you stay clean - and when you're clean, you can be covered.

*Romans 6:23 - For the wages of sin is death; but the gift of God is eternal life through Jesus Christ our Lord (KJV).*

That's why it is important, when you pray, to ask God to forgive you if you've offended Him knowingly or unknowingly. Do this every day and receive His forgiveness so that you can draw strength to live. Didn't Jesus teach us to pray, *"Do not lead us into temptation, but deliver us from the evil one"?* Yes! So we need to pray every day, "Lord, today, give me bread; today, deliver me; today, keep me from the evil one."

*James 4:7* says, *"Submit yourselves therefore to God..." (KJV).* That means to align your life under the Lordship of Christ. There is a wonderful kind of boldness that comes from walking in obedience to God. The Bible tells us that people who have sin in their lives are paranoid, but that those who walk in integrity have a holy boldness.

*Proverbs 28:1* says, *"The wicked flee when no one pursues, But the righteous are bold as a lion."* They refuse to run from their enemies, but like David against Goliath, they run toward their enemies, fully expecting victory. *James 4:7* continues and says, *"Resist the devil."* That means there is warfare involved and that you will have to do some pushing. The word resist doesn't mean just submit to God and say, "Go away" to the devil. He will not be shooed away like a fly! You must actively resist him until he understands that you will not back off.

As you resist the devil, your learning curve might look something like this. The first battle you go through might require that you resist for months. You may go through a situation in which the devil is saying, "I'll just wear him or her out. I will wear that person out!"

You resist and keep resisting; you start submitting to God and continue the two-pronged weapon of submitting and resisting. Whatever you are up against will finally break, and when it does, your faith will be built up. Then, the next time you are in a similar battle, you can win it in a month. The next time it will be a week, and the next time it will only be hours. Pretty soon, you won't have those types of battles any more. Submit to God, resist the devil and he will flee from you *(James 4:7)*.

I love to read about the faith of the Canaanite woman in *Matthew 15.*

> *Matthew 15: 22-28* - A Canaanite woman...came to him,
> crying out, "Lord, Son of David, have mercy on me! My
> daughter is suffering terribly from demon-possession." **23**
> *Jesus did not answer a word. So his disciples came to him*
> *and urged him, "Send her away, for she keeps crying out*
> *after us." **24** He answered, "I was sent only to the lost*
> *sheep of Israel." **25** The woman came and knelt before him.*
> *"Lord, help me!" she said. **26** He replied, "It is not right to*
> *take the children's bread and toss it to their dogs." **27** "Yes,*
> *Lord," she said, "but even the dogs eat the crumbs that fall*
> *from their masters' table." **28** Then Jesus answered,*
> *"Woman, you have great faith! Your request is granted."*
> *And her daughter was healed from that very hour (NIV).*

Although she was an outsider - a Gentile with
no claim to covenant promises - this Canaanite
woman continued to press Jesus for her daughter's
deliverance. She is only one of two people Jesus
described as having great faith! She refused to be
denied; she persisted and eventually received her miracle.

*Psalm 25:19-21* states, *"See how my enemies*
*have increased and how fiercely they hate me! Guard*
*my life and rescue me; let me not be put to shame, for*
*I take refuge in you. May* **integrity** *and uprightness*
*protect me, because my hope is in you"* (NIV -
emphasis added). Look also at *Psalm 84:11, "For the*
*Lord God is a sun and shield; the Lord bestows favor*
*and honor; no good thing does He withhold from*
*those whose walk is blameless"* (NIV).

It is clear that the Lord is a shield to those who walk uprightly, and integrity within us will build a shield around us. Also, *Proverbs 16:17* tells us, *"God's people avoid evil ways, and they protect themselves by watching where they go"(CEV)*. Let's walk in integrity by avoiding evil ways and keep ourselves protected by paying attention to the things we do, think and say.

## Intercession

There is powerful protection in intercession. Our prayers and the prayers of other people help keep us protected, and likewise, we help keep our brothers and sisters protected as we pray for them. God says there is a reward if we pray (*Matthew 6:6; Hebrews 10:35*). Look what the Lord says in *Ezekiel 22:30*, *"I sought for a man among them, that should make up the hedge, and stand in the gap before me for the land, that I should not destroy it: but I found none" (KJV)*.

> *Matthew 6:6* - *But you, when you pray, go into your room, and when you have shut your door, pray to your Father who is in the secret place; and your Father who sees in secret will reward you openly.*
> *Hebrews 10:35* - *Keep on being brave! It will bring you great rewards (CEV).*

God's invitation to us is to stand in the gaps and learn to build hedges through prayer and intercession. So how do we say yes to Him? First, let's find out what a gap is.

Biblically, a gap was a break in the wall of protection around a city, an invasion point whereby an enemy could gain access. Gaps, in terms of intercessory prayer, are weak spots or entry points in our lives where the enemy can attack us. We must understand the significance of broken hedges. The Bible warns us of broken hedges or gaps in our wall.

*Ecclesiastes 10:8* says that whoever breaks a hedge, a serpent will bite him. This passage warns us of two things: first, on the other side of the hedge, the enemy is waiting to afflict us. Secondly, he is looking for weak spots in our walls so that he can gain entry into our lives and enlarge his base of operations. Once the enemy has access, he continues working to enlarge the gap and destroy the hedges protecting you.

Our enemy is invisible, but we must remember that this unseen foe always leaves very visible tracks! It is easy to follow the trail of destruction and see where the enemy has been. I especially like the way *The Living Bible* paraphrases *Psalm 89:40, 41, "You have broken down the walls protecting him and laid in ruins every fort defending him. Everyone who comes along has robbed him while his neighbors mock."* When hedges are broken, we are robbed, and our enemies mock.

I have found that many people are unsuccessful in warring effectively in prayer because they do not understand broken hedges, do not recognize the gaps, or do not know how to spot where the enemy is breaking in. They feel overwhelmed because they are seemingly being attacked from every side. If we can quickly discern where the enemy is trying to invade, we can immediately go to war in the gap or break through and stop the invasion before it gets out of control!

God has called us not only to stand in the gaps, but also to build protective hedges. Are you tired of being robbed and tormented? Once you learn to stand in the invasion point and push your enemies back, you can begin to learn to build protective hedges around yourself.

If we pray, we can actually build our own protective fallout shelter through our prayers. We can go into that place and be safe. We can construct a dwelling place in prayer, hide there and experience the kind of protection *Psalm 91:7* describes, which says, *"A thousand may fall at your side, and ten thousand at your right hand; but it shall not come near you."* We must pray fervently and relentlessly for others and for ourselves - because prayer helps us stay protected and through intercession, we build hedges.

# Building A Mental Prayer Hedge

## Chapter Five

As I have prayed over a number of years and understood the hedges mentioned above, the Lord has taught me to pray for hedges around seven specific areas for myself, my family, my work and my possessions. I believe that most, if not all of these areas, will apply to you as well. Though a person's relationship with God cannot be reduced to a formula, I do believe you will find the prayer pattern in the following pages an effective strategy for your life when it is inspired, empowered and guided by the Holy Spirit.

## A Mental Hedge

The first aspect of our lives around which we can pray a hedge is our minds. We can ask the Lord for a shield of protection around our thought life. When we are under attack, the first line of assault is usually our minds; we become confused. The enemy will overtake us when we cannot think as we need to, when we are overwhelmed, frustrated or our thoughts are in disarray. When our minds are under attack and the enemy is taunting us, the first thing we need to do is pray, "Lord, I command my thoughts to come into order."

We must have divine strategy, and we must have the mind of Christ in every situation. Our minds need to be disciplined so that we can pray focused, persistent prayers. We must be able to take every thought captive in the name of Jesus. Getting the mind of the Lord may require praying for a while, but eventually, it will happen.

The cycle usually looks something like this. The enemy will look for a weak spot in our lives and continue to attack it. If he is allowed to break through, he will torment us (*Ecclesiastes.10:8*). His goal is to rob our fruit and mock us (*Ps.89:40-41*). But most importantly, he wants to establish strongholds in our lives. If we are tormented and robbed long enough, we begin to believe there is no hope, and this is just the way it was meant to be.

**Ecclesiastes 10:8** - *He who digs a pit will fall into it, And whoever breaks through a wall will be bitten by a serpent.*

**Psalms 89:40-41-** *You have broken through all his walls and reduced his strongholds to ruins. 41 All who pass by have plundered him; he has become the scorn of his neighbors (NIV).*

It is important to know that we first need to pray that the strongholds in our minds will be torn down. *2 Corinthians 10:4* says, *"For the weapons of our warfare are not carnal, but mighty through God to the pulling down of strong holds"* (KJV). A stronghold is a "house of thoughts" that Satan builds inside our minds.

Let me share with you how Satan constructs a stronghold. He first drops off lumber; he just dumps the substance of the stronghold in your mind. If you do not recognize that he is trespassing and command him to get his trash off your property, then it stays there in the form of random thoughts - thoughts that should have been taken captive but were not.

Soon, the enemy begins to take pieces of that lumber and gives you ideas. With every idea inspired by the enemy, another board gets nailed into place as the stronghold takes shape in your mind. If you still don't get angry and burn up the lumber, ideas become concepts, and pretty soon the concepts become strongholds. They become like a reality, like an entire house that has been built in your mind. You do not even question it.

It all starts with one wrong thought that turns into a whole system of thoughts and responses that occupy a great deal of space in your mind. But the Bible says the weapons we have will demolish these. God's Word is like a heavenly bulldozer in your mind that pulls down strongholds. Following is a list of common strongholds:

» Strongholds of division

» Strongholds of poverty

» Strongholds of unbelief

» Strongholds of infirmity

» Strongholds of unforgiveness

» Strongholds of sexual lust

» Strongholds of jealousy or envy

» Strongholds of inferiority

» Strongholds of religious tradition

» Strongholds of materialism

Secondly, we need to pray for transformation through the renewing of our minds. God does the transforming, but we need to take responsibility for making sure that we are vigilant over our minds and that we guard our thoughts aggressively.

I cannot count the times in my life when my thoughts were like birds flying in and out of a tree - all sorts of random, undisciplined thoughts came and went in my mind. I had to learn to pray, "Lord, I bring every thought into captivity. God, throw a net over my thought life. Lord, throw a net over it and capture every thought." Then I learned to confess God's Word, "I have the mind of Christ." I said to the Lord, "Your Word says, 'Let this mind be in you that was also in Christ.'" I now say, "Let that mind be in me. I confess that I have the mind of Christ. I still feel confused and frustrated, but I believe that I have the mind of Christ."

I then begin to pray like this: "Lord, I come against these random thoughts that not only run through my mind, but the minds of the people in the church I pastor. I see them falling into unbelief; I see them allowing division in their relationships. Oh Lord, pull those strongholds down in the name of Jesus!"

As I travel and minister throughout the body of Christ, I see so much unbelief which is only one example of a stronghold. Does unbelief or any other stronghold come from the Holy Spirit? Do they come from reading the Word? Do strongholds get built as a result of worship or from hanging out with Jesus? Where do they come from? You know - they come from the pit of hell.

Once that load of lumber lands in your mind, if you do not get rid of it, the enemy will build a house of thoughts that will destroy you. Let us determine not to rest until the strongholds in our minds are bulldozed in the name of Jesus. We start by going after them with a hammer, but soon the Holy Spirit bursts on the scene with the heavy machinery. He is our Helper, and He comes to help us demolish strongholds and to transform us by the renewing of our minds.

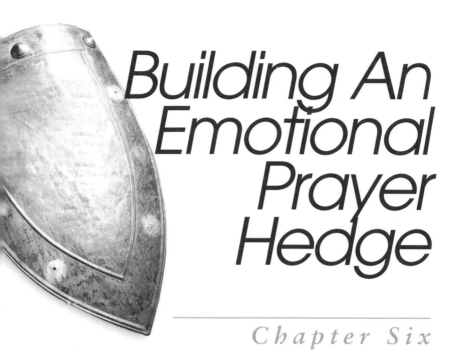

# Building An Emotional Prayer Hedge

## Chapter Six

Do your emotions ever get the best of you? Do you ever feel that your life is guided by them or that you make decisions based on how you feel? In warfare the second area that must be brought into alignment is our emotions. The Lord has taught me to pray a hedge around my emotions. Why? In my case, I needed a hedge around my emotions because I wrestled with fear. I have been amazed by the number of people who are afraid of something - illnesses, accidents or finances falling apart. They may fear something happening to their children or a whole list of other things.

There are at least two forces in the kingdom of darkness that draw demonic spirits: one is fear and the other is hatred (which includes unforgiveness and bitterness). Fear and hatred compose the atmosphere of the demonic kingdom, and I have observed that almost everyone who struggles with emotional or spiritual problems does so for one of these two reasons. The Bible says, *"For God has not given us the spirit of fear" (2 Timothy 1:7).*

Fear is a spirit. Fear is accompanied by torment. Since God has given us the spirit of power and love and of a sound mind, we are not to receive fear. Your brain can and will say to you, "You really need to be afraid," but when you are walking in power, love and a sound mind, your heart will say, "I'm not afraid." Indeed, it is possible to be besieged by fear in your mind, but full of faith in your heart.

There have been countless times in my life when I encounter certain situations and my mind says to me, "Man, you really should be scared." Every natural sensor is blaring, "Be afraid! Be afraid!" Still, my heart is able to trust in God. We need to learn to pray an emotional hedge around ourselves and our loved ones just as David and Joshua did.

When David was overwhelmed and crying out for deliverance, he said, *"But I pray to you, O Lord, in the time of your favor; in your great love, O God, answer me with your sure salvation. Rescue me from the mire, do not let me sink; deliver me from those who hate me, from the deep waters. Do not let the floodwaters engulf me or the depths swallow me up or the pit close its mouth over me. Answer me, O Lord, out of the goodness of your love; in your great mercy turn to me" (Psalm 69:13-16, NIV).*

"*Have I not commanded you, Joshua? Be strong and courageous. Do not be terrified, or full of fear; do not be discouraged, for the Lord your God will be with you wherever you go" (Joshua 1:9, paraphrased).* If you want to be a person who takes land for God, you cannot be fearful and discouraged. What are the two things we fight against all the time? Fear and discouragement. Any time you are moving forward, what do you think the devil will throw at you - fear and/or discouragement, which means to lose your courage. We must be strong and courageous as God's people, and that is why it is so important to pray a hedge around your emotions.

How can you do this in a practical way? Pray something like this: "Lord, let the walls be built around me emotionally. I'm not going to be faint-hearted. I'm not going to be a coward. I'm not always going to be tentative or anxious. I'm not always going to live under discouragement."

What does the Bible say about David? David encouraged himself in the Lord his God (*I Samuel* 30:6). We must learn how to draw courage from the

Lord our God. There is a place in prayer where we can do just that - where we can dip deeply into the well of courage and draw bucket after bucket. When we do, we come out of the prayer closet strong in the Lord and in the power of His might.

*I Samuel 30:6 Now David was greatly distressed, for the people spoke of stoning him, because the soul of all the people was grieved, every man for his sons and his daughters. But David strengthened himself in the LORD his God.*

We can emerge from our times with the Lord in strength, speaking blessing instead of looking for somebody to pat us on the back and build us up. People alone cannot build us up. We must be built up through prayer and refuse to be discouraged! We must be strong and courageous.

You were meant to be courageous not discouraged. If you find yourself discouraged, how did you lose your courage? Where did you lose your gumption and your grit? It's time to recover courage. It's time for you to arise and to be strong. Pray to overcome emotionally. Pray to overcome fear. Pray to overcome anger and unforgiveness. Pray to overcome discouragement and depression. Pray to overcome apathy. Keep praying to overcome whatever your particular struggle is, and then think about the following scriptures.

*Isaiah 41:10* says: *"So do not fear."* Why? *"I am with you."* Isn't that good news? God is with you! The verse continues, *"Do not be dismayed."* Why? *"I am your God. I will strengthen you and help you; I will uphold you with my righteous right hand."* Verse 11 begins, *"All who rage against you...."* Do you see them raging? Are the veins popping out of their necks? Are people or situations threatening you?

Hear what God says in the rest of that verse, *"All who rage against you will surely be ashamed and disgraced; those who oppose you will be as nothing and perish. Though you search for your enemies, you will not find them. Those who wage war against you will be as nothing at all. For I am the Lord, your God, who takes hold of your right hand and says to you, Do not fear; I will help you"* (NIV). Now, there is peace. Our Father, our Papa, is our Helper. With Him on our side, we do not fear.

*Psalm 66:10-12* says, *"For you, O God, tested us; you refined us like silver. You brought us into prison and laid burdens on our backs. You let men ride over our heads; we went through fire and water, but you brought us out to a place of abundance"* (NIV). Wow! Is that awesome? Begin now to pray a hedge of protection over your emotions and allow the Lord to lead you through - yes, all the way through - and deal with those areas in your life and bring you into a place of abundance and freedom.

# Building A Physical Prayer Hedge

*Chapter Seven*

When someone or something is threatening you physically, pray a hedge of protection. I have had numerous threats on my life, and I have had to learn how to pray a hedge of protection around my life and the lives of my family.

I recently visited someone in a psychiatric unit. Many people in psychiatric units are spiritually oppressed. As I was waiting to see the person I needed to visit, a man I had never seen before approached me. He was obviously heavily medicated, but when he looked at me, he seemed to snap into perfect clarity and said, "All preachers are liars." I found his comment unusual because there was no way he could have known I was a preacher - I was dressed in jeans and a polo shirt!

I responded, "What did you say?"

"All preachers are liars." Then he continued, "But you're not a liar."

I said, "You're right. I'm not a liar."
I knew I was talking to a demon.

And he said, "But they keep telling me to blow up the church!"

I looked him squarely in the eye and I said, "You are not going to blow up anything! Do you hear me? You are not going to blow up anything. Now be still, in Jesus' name! Get out of here, in the name of Jesus!"

At that, the man faded back into his drug-induced stupor.

Demons attempt to intimidate you and make you afraid. We are not to allow the enemy to do that. He operates through fear, so we must pray hedges of protection around ourselves. Our times are in the hands of the Lord. *Psalm 31:15* says that our times - our lives - are in His hands. No one is going to take us out prematurely. We will live every single day that God has ordained.

*Psalms 31: 15 - My times are in your hands; deliver me from my enemies and from those who pursue me (NIV).*

*Psalm 103:2-4* says, *"Bless the Lord, O my soul and forget not all His benefits."* What are those benefits? *"He forgives all your iniquities; He heals all your diseases; He redeems your life from destruction."* And then what does *Psalm 91* say? The Lord will save us from secret traps. We need to ask Him for specific protection in the following areas of potential destruction or secret traps.

## Accidents and Disasters

We can pray a protective hedge around ourselves to protect us against accidents and disasters. This is an especially wise prayer to pray before and during travel. Before I take a trip, I pray, "Lord, thank You for a physical hedge of protection. Thank You that I'm safe from accidents and disasters."

I once taught on hedges of protection at a church. As I was teaching, one man really took the message seriously and the next day applied it to his life. On his way to work that morning, he was praying and asking the Lord to put up various hedges. He began to pray a hedge around his toddler son, Tom, "Lord, put a hedge around Tom." As he prayed, he felt that the Lord said to him, "Just keep praying more for your son. Ask Me to commission angels to protect him."

He continued, "Lord, protect Tom. Send angels to protect Tom and keep him safe...." When he arrived at work, his boss approached him and said with an ashen face, "Go straight to the hospital. Tom's been in an accident."

He rushed to the hospital and asked his wife what had happened. She reported that Tom had been playing on a table and had somehow gotten a curtain cord caught around his neck. He fell off the table and hung by the curtain cord long enough for his oxygen to be cut off before the mother found him. When the mother arrived at the hospital, doctors told her that his oxygen had been cut off so long that they were not sure they could save his life. Even if they could, his brain would be damaged.

So the parents prayed, and the father understood why the Lord had asked him to keep praying protection for Tom. After what seemed like an eternity, the doctor came out and said to the man and his wife, "All I can say is that there must be an angel watching over this kid. There is absolutely nothing wrong with this boy but a little mark." Prayer makes a difference. It defies the odds, and the effectual, fervent prayer of a righteous person really does avail much.

*James 5:16 - Confess your faults one to another, and pray one for another, that ye may be healed. The effectual fervent prayer of a righteous man availeth much (KJV).*

## Attacks and Assassination

We need to pray for protection from attacks and assassination. This is a powerful way to pray for those in the military, or law enforcement. Additionally, pray for firefighters, rescue workers, or anyone whose life is in harm's way.

> *Ecclesiastes 9:12* - *"No one knows what will happen next. Like a fish caught in a net, or a bird caught in a trap, people are trapped by evil when it suddenly falls on them"* (NCV).
>
> *Psalm 142:3-5* - *"For I am overwhelmed, and you alone know the way I should turn. Wherever I go, my enemies have set traps for me. I look for someone to come and help me, but no one gives me a passing thought! No one will help me; no one cares a bit what happens to me. **Then I pray to you, O Lord. I say, 'You are my place of refuge. You are all I really want in life'"** (NLT).
>
> *Psalm 25:15* - *"I always look to you, because **you rescue me from every trap"** (CEV) .

I once spoke at a conference in Portland, Oregon, and someone told me that in World War I, the U.S. Army's 91st Brigade, who fought in France, prayed and recited the 91st Psalm every day. Sometimes *Psalm 91* is called "The Soldier's Psalm." The 91st Brigade fought in three of the bloodiest battles in World War I, and other units who fought in those battles suffered the loss or wounding of as many as 90% of their soldiers. But the 91st Brigade sustained no combat-related casualties - not a single war-related injury or death. The Lord was their strongest weapon.

Dennis Balcombe, a modern missionary to China, shared the testimony of a friend who served with him in Vietnam. They were in a firefight. An enemy round struck Dennis' friend in the chest. As he lay on the jungle floor, he realized he was not bleeding. He felt in the area of his chest where the bullet hit. Amazingly, it had not struck him but had pierced the Bible that he carried in his chest pocket. The miracle is this - the bullet penetrated all the way through the New Testament and the point of the bullet stopped at Psalm 91! God's Word is powerfully miraculous to those who believe!

More recently, I heard this story from a woman in our church:

*In October 2001, my brother was deployed to Afghanistan to fight the United States' war on terrorism. In March 2002, the most intense ground battle of the war in Afghanistan took place. My brother landed in the Shah-e-Kot valley, and he and his comrades immediately came under enemy fire. They had discovered one of the largest, fiercest concentrations of Al-Qaeda and Taliban and were suddenly engaged in an eighteen-hour firefight that was as brutal as it was unexpected.*

*The terrorist fighters had the advantage of a mountain stronghold riddled with tunnels and caves in which to hide. The American soldiers had no way out. As the day wore on, air support sent the enemy scurrying into the caves, giving U.S. forces an opportunity to reposition. When the aircraft departed, intense enemy gunfire resumed. Under attack from every side, running low on ammunition and food, with many men wounded, the troops held their ground until most of the enemy was defeated. Through skill, stamina and a small dip in the terrain (known as "the bowl"), every U.S. soldier lived.*

*I remembered Pastor Servello's teaching series on Psalm 91. He taught us how to pray hedges around our families. He told us a story about the World War I brigade who had prayed Psalm 91 and had not lost a single soldier. I sent several copies of Psalm 91 to my brother for himself and for his colleagues and told them to read it prayerfully every day. Whether they did or not, I do not know; but I prayed a hedge of protection over my brother and his men daily. All of the soldiers made it out of the Shah-e-Kot valley alive, and my brother was quoted in Time magazine as saying, "We put the capital 'M' in 'miracle'."*

*I give all the glory to God for His faithfulness, which kept my brother and the other soldiers safe.*

Several years ago, during a time when I was especially focused on praying a hedge of protection against attacks and assassinations, a strange man walked into our church service and tried to approach the platform. When the ushers stopped him, he exploded with anger and was quickly escorted out of the room.

About a week later, two detectives from the Utica Police Department came to our church and began asking us questions about this man. When we asked them what he had done, they informed us that he had barricaded himself inside a local motel room and waited for the housekeeper to arrive for her daily cleaning duties. When she walked into the room, he pointed a gun at her and threatened to kill her! Somehow, she was able to call the police. They arrived quickly, surrounded the room, and called for him to drop his gun and come out quietly. He then threatened to kill the officers while walking toward them with his gun pointed at them. Before he could shoot them, he was shot and killed.

We asked why they were questioning us, and they informed us that his room was filled with material from our church. They said we were very fortunate that he did not try to harm anyone at the church service, which seemed to be his intent. I knew again that God had protected us against the devil's assignment!

The Word of God is powerful; prayer is powerful. This is why I encourage you so strongly to read and pray *Psalm 91* every day.

## Infirmity and Disease

We also need to pray for protection against infirmity and disease. We must continually resist the spirit of infirmity and disease. Let's say that you or someone in your house is sick. Start to submit to God. Speak the truth of God's Word and begin to resist the devil with the Word.

Put the Word on your body and speak to those spirits of infirmity and disease saying, "Get out of my body and get out of my home in the name of Jesus! I claim health for myself and I thank you, God, for a protective hedge around this home. Sickness will not dwell in my home! There's a hedge built around me, my family and all that I have. Get out of my house in the name of Jesus! God's protective hedge is around me."

## Pray That God's Healing Power Is Released

Pray that God's power is released for physical healing, emotional healing, the healing of relationships, and any type of healing you or someone around you needs.

A woman in Dallas received the news that her mother had been diagnosed with an aggressive type of cancer and that the prognosis was grim. Because the mother lived in another state, she needed to move in with the daughter for several weeks during a series of visits to M.D. Anderson Cancer Center in Houston and while she recovered from surgery.

The daughter understood how powerful it is to have the Spirit of God living within us. Every night while the mother slept, the daughter laid hands on her mother and prayed for God's healing power to be released. At every opportunity, she prayed and continued to believe that His power was being released.

Within a few months, the mother had experienced a healing miracle. Because of the type of cancer with which she had been stricken, doctors and nurses marveled at her complete recovery. That woman, in her mid-seventies, was soon able to enjoy her favorite activities again - including eighteen holes of golf five days a week!

Another healing miracle took place within our church. I'll let Sharon Sweet tell you about it in her own words:

*On October 4, 1995, at age 42, I was exhausted, weak, had no desire to eat, experienced body aches and found it very difficult to go up and down stairs. My head pounded and my body went from hot to cold in a matter of seconds. I called the doctor and went to his office for an exam and blood work. Within several hours after I returned home, the doctor's office called and said I needed to get to the hospital right away for a sonogram of my organs. The nurse said that my liver levels were elevated to a very dangerous point. After the sonogram and a second blood test, on October 5, 1995, I was diagnosed with Hepatitis B. Formerly, this form of hepatitis was called "serum hepatitis," which is commonly caused by infected blood or blood products. Food or water contaminated by feces can infect individuals with this disease, and it can be spread by ear piercing, tattooing, manicures (un-sterilized instruments), or intravenous drug use. Hepatitis B is called a "killer" disease, and children ages 10 and under can die from it.*

*Unhappy with the results of our local doctor in Ilion, NY, my husband made an appointment for me with a disease control specialist at The Infectious Disease Associates of Syracuse located in Syracuse, NY. After more blood work and another examination, the doctor confirmed the previous diagnosis, Hepatitis B. She then told us what to expect—that it could lead to cirrhosis of the liver, cancer of the liver or, down the road, the need for a possible liver transplant. Untreated Hepatitis causes severe liver damage and may result in coma due to liver failure. It can also cause death. Nothing could be done for the illness in my body; there were no drugs or treatments she could prescribe.*

*The doctor told us to go home and make me as comfortable as possible, and that time would dictate the outcome. My husband and our four children each had to be tested for the disease, and they each received the 3-injection series to protect them.*

*I did not receive the diagnosis! I told people, "They say I have it, but I do not receive it!" I knew in my heart that God was not finished with me and that there was so much more for me to do. So, day and night, I lay on the couch and listened to healing Scriptures on audiotape and to worship songs. I believed God's Word, which says that He is my healer. I delved into the Word of God like never before and now know that the Word is so key to our lives. It does bring life! I stood solidly on two scriptures. "He was wounded for my transgressions, He was bruised for my iniquities; the chastisement of my peace was upon him, and by His stripes I am healed" (Isaiah 53:5), and "I shall not die, but live, and declare the works of the Lord" (Psalm 118:17). Many people from the church came to our house and prayed for me, and the entire church came together in unity to stand in the gap with us.*

*I began to get stronger and began to resume my daily activities. I had a follow-up appointment with the disease control doctor on December 11, 1995. She was so surprised by the results of my blood test that she re-ran the test. She told my husband and me that, "I don't understand it, but the blood work came back normal and there are no signs of Hepatitis B." The doctor went on to say that had I not been labeled with the disease, I would be able to donate blood. The test also showed I was immune to all three* types of hepatitis—A, B and C—and the doctor then said, "You are healed!" She reported that my liver was normal, and she could not understand what happened. My response was easy, "My God healed me, and my God not only heals, He gives dividends too!"

In December of 2003, I will have been healed for eight years. I am still healthy, with no disease and a very healthy liver! I love to pray for the sick and watch them receive their miracles too! For that, I give God all the glory!

There are a lot of scriptures on healing, and just a few of them are listed here so that by reading them, your faith for healing can be strengthened.

*Isaiah 53: 5* - But He was wounded for our transgressions, He was bruised for our iniquities; The chastisement for our peace was upon Him, And by His stripes we are healed.
*Jeremiah 17:14* - Heal me, O LORD , and I will be healed; save me and I will be saved, for you are the one I praise (NIV).
*Jeremiah 30:17* - But I will restore you to health and heal your wounds, declares the LORD..."
*Psalms 103:2* - Bless the LORD, O my soul, And forget not all His benefits: 3Who forgives all your iniquities, Who heals all your diseases.
*Psalms 107:20* - He sent forth his word and healed them; he rescued them from the grave (NIV).

*continued on 74*

*Matthew 8:16* - *When evening had come, they brought to Him many who were demon-possessed. And He cast out the spirits with a word, and healed all who were sick, 17that it might be fulfilled which was spoken by Isaiah the prophet, saying: "He Himself took our infirmities And bore our sicknesses."*

*Acts 4:30* - *Stretch out your hand to heal and perform miraculous signs and wonders through the name of your holy servant Jesus" (NIV).*

*I Peter 2:24* - *He personally carried away our sins in his own body on the cross so we can be dead to sin and live for what is right. You have been healed by his wounds (NLT).*

# Building A Spiritual Prayer Hedge

## Chapter Eight

We need to pray a spiritual hedge. In the supernatural realm, spirits are released for the purpose of attacking us spiritually. We need to pray for protection against evil spirits and deception as we read in *1 Timothy 4:1,"The Spirit clearly says that in later times some will abandon the faith and follow deceiving spirits and things taught by demons" (NIV).*

Most of us have probably seen the television commercials broadcast by the Church of Jesus Christ of Latter Day Saints, otherwise known as the Mormons. These advertisements are so slick - using the name of Jesus and offering free Bibles - that you would almost think they are promoting a Christian group. At the close of the commercial, however, they mention an addition to the Bible - the Book of Mormon! My friend, there is no standard of life and truth besides God's Word! It needs no additional offers! Other so called "sacred texts" do not contain the holy, inspired, life-giving Word of the Lord, and they lead people into deception.

One reason we pray a spiritual hedge around ourselves and our churches is so that we cannot and will not be deceived. We live in an age of great deception where people are taken captive daily by false belief systems and strange religions. We want to stay in Christ, to know and obey the truth of God's Word and to live in intimate communion with the Lord. We have to stay protected against everything that exalts itself against the knowledge of God.

I was praying this prayer for spiritual protection long before I ever told anyone about it, but one night, my wife dreamed that she and I were walking through a room and the people in our church were following us. We went through a room filled with small snakes, serpents. In the dream the people of the church were walking through that room stomping on the serpents and cutting their heads off. Meanwhile, I walked ahead into another room where two large serpents were hiding in the dark. As I took a step, they lunged at me ready to bite. As they lunged, I took another step just in time, and they missed me. In the dream she kept saying to me, "Be careful. Be careful."

I turned to her and said, "I'm not afraid. I know I'm not afraid, and I'll tell you why: I pray a hedge of protection around myself spiritually. Those serpents are not going to bite me."

> *Psalms 140: 4-7 - Protect me, LORD, from cruel and brutal enemies, who want to destroy me. 5 Those proud people have hidden traps and nets to catch me as I walk. 6 You, LORD, are my God! Please listen to my prayer. 7 You have the power to save me, and you keep me safe in every battle (CEV).*

So many people live their Christian lives walking merrily along until, "Bump!" They get hit in the back of the head with some kind of attack. Then they say, "I never saw that coming." How long are we going to continue being blindsided by the enemy? Until we start to realize that we can pray and have the mind of the Lord *before* things begin to happen. So I pray this way, "Holy Spirit, put a spiritual hedge around me, around the church, around my family. Holy Spirit, we want to know You."

Every day tell Him, "I want to know you. I want to commune with You. Anything I've done to grieve You - I repent for that. I just want to commune and know You, Holy Spirit; I honor You. Holy Spirit please keep me steps ahead of the enemy." I really do pray those words: "Keep me steps ahead of the enemy." When my wife had that dream, God again was confirming to me that He was hearing and answering my prayers, indeed keeping me steps ahead of the enemy.

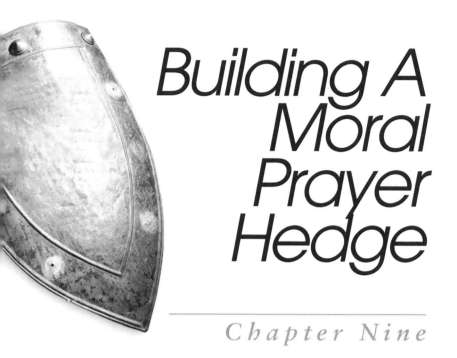

# Building A Moral Prayer Hedge

## Chapter Nine

The Lord also taught me to pray a moral hedge. Oh, how we need a moral hedge around us! We are God's people, and we are not going to fall into the ways of the world.

Several years ago, a large church experienced a Toronto-style revival, but the pastor was thrown out of the church. The people took the pulpit he preached from and destroyed it because the man had numerous affairs - one that lasted six years - and did not want to repent. He was not even willing to repent when confronted with this ongoing sin and responded instead that he was only sorry he got caught.

There are spirits of filthiness, and they attack the character of individuals, pervert people's thoughts and destroy their morals. These spirits are aggressive against our young people, especially trying to get into dating relationships. These spirits of filthiness want to overtake us, often luring men into pornography and women into fantasy. They use books and movies and magazines, and they take maximum advantage of the internet as they seek to influence and destroy us. We can pray a moral hedge around ourselves and those we love: "God, I declare that I am protected, in the name of Jesus. These filthy things will not come upon me. Lord, keep me pure and holy."

The Bible also says that if we pray anything according to His will, we can know that He hears us. *I Thessalonians 3:13; 4:7* and *1 Peter 1:15,16* tell us that it is the will of God that we be holy. When I pray, I say, "God, it is Your will that I be holy, and as I pray this, I know You hear me. You're going to make me holy." *Psalm 91* tells us that a thousand may fall on this side and ten thousand on that side, but that it will not come nigh your dwelling place. What does that mean for us? We are not going to succumb to the filth and perversion of the world around us.

*I Thessalonians 3:13* - *So that He may establish your hearts blameless in holiness before our God and Father at the coming of our Lord Jesus Christ with all His saints.*
*I Thessalonians 4:7* - *For God did not call us to be impure, but to live a holy life (NIV).*
*I Peter 1: 15-16* - *But as he which hath called you is holy, so be ye holy in all manner of conversation; 16 Because it is written, Be ye holy; for I am holy (KJV).*

The Lord will help us stay morally pure. We are going to have good marriages and raise children who are pure. Our homes are not going to be bitten by adultery, homosexuality, perversion and child abuse. That is not what goes on in kingdom homes, so we pray and ask the Lord to keep us protected morally.

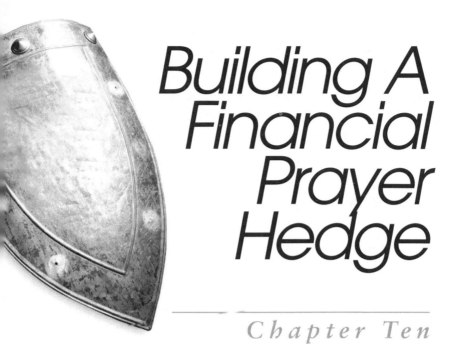

# Building A Financial Prayer Hedge

*Chapter Ten*

We can pray a hedge of protection around our finances. Have you ever known someone whose money bag seemed to be filled with holes? People in that situation seem to never be able to get their paychecks into the bank before the money is spent and gone. These people never have enough money, and their entire financial situation is one big tangled mess.

In years of ministry, I have dealt with people who make a substantial living but live like paupers. I have dealt with others who do not earn as much but are living very well. So what is happening to those who cannot hold onto or manage their money? In some cases ignorance or lack of discipline may be to blame. In many cases people are being robbed by the enemy who only comes to "steal, kill and destroy."

One of the foundational presuppositions of these prayer principles is that your life is in order and you are walking in the power of God's Spirit and in obedience to the truth of His Word, which includes the area of financial giving. The Bible is full of promises to those who give. *Proverbs 3:9 says, "Honor the LORD with your wealth, with the first fruits of all your crops; 10 then your barns will be filled to overflowing, and your vats will brim over with new wine" (NIV).*

Let's look now in Malachi where we find another of God's powerful promises. *Malachi 3:10-12 says, "Bring all the tithes into the storehouse, that there may be food in My house, And try Me now in this," Says the LORD of hosts, "If I will not open for you the windows of heaven And pour out for you such blessing That there will not be room enough to receive it. 11 "And I will rebuke the devourer for your sakes, So that he will not destroy the fruit of your ground, Nor shall the vine fail to bear fruit for you in the field," Says the LORD of hosts; 12 "And all nations will call you blessed, For you will be a delightful land," Says the LORD of hosts."*

There is supernatural power released as we

begin to give. The resources of Heaven begin to over-run our natural limitations, and we experience break-through. God opens the Heavens for us in blessing and places His angels around us. As we honor the Lord with our giving, He has promised to rebuke the devourer, or that which breaks in and eats up our increase.

You may be surprised to learn that giving actually builds a hedge around you - a hedge of blessing. *Isaiah 32:8* tells us, *"But good men will be generous to others and will be blessed of God for all they do"(LB).*

As we discover in the book of Psalms, our generosity must include giving to the poor. In *Psalm 41:1-3* it says, *"Blessed is he who considers the poor; The LORD will deliver him in time of trouble. 2 The LORD will preserve him and keep him alive, And he will be blessed on the earth; You will not deliver him to the will of his enemies. 3 The LORD will strengthen him on his bed of illness; You will sustain him on his sickbed."*

There are a number of promises contained in these verses:
1. God promises to bless those who are kind and help the poor.
   *Proverbs 22:9 - The LORD blesses everyone who freely gives food to the poor (CEV).*
2. God delivers them when they are in trouble.

3. God preserves those who help the poor.
   Preserve, in God's Word, means
   to build a hedge around you - to guard you.
4. God publicly honors them. What we do in
   secret God declares in the marketplace.
5. God delivers them from the power of their
   enemies. When you give to the poor, not
   only are the plots and plans of your enemies
   foiled – you are *supernaturally* protected.
6. God comforts and heals them when they are
   sick.

Blessing begins to overtake us from every side as we use our resources to extend the kingdom of God.

If you are a responsible steward and your financial activities are in line with the Word of God, and you're still being robbed, you must learn to pray a protective hedge around your finances.

Norman and Diane Bunce are dear friends of ours from the Catskill Region of New York. Here is their testimony in their own words: "As Norman and I began to read your book, we realized the importance of praying hedges around our family, business, properties, etc. There was a time when it seemed as though a lot of business deals were not being completed but were being aborted before we could close. We know it was Satan buffeting us. We also had two rental properties that were not rented and the season was getting late for rentals. When we prayed a hedge around our business and our properties, within two weeks both of our rental properties were rented, and real estate rentals and sales in our business began to soar. Now we pray hedges around our family, finances, business, health, church, etc. for God's divine protection that cannot be penetrated by the enemy."

Again, a key principle relative to these promises of protection, is that your life is in order and you are walking with God according to the truth of His Word. When that is the case, God is our sure defense.

In 1990, our church moved to Utica, New York. God had blessed us, and we were able to build a large new building for the church. However, we began to experience financial problems from the first month we began to minister in the city. We continued to have financial problems for the next nine years! We never finished one year in the black; we were continually thousands of dollars in the red.

We operated very responsibly and paid all our bills on time. We were very generous to those in need and in our missions giving. Nevertheless, we could never seem to break the stranglehold of the spirit of poverty.

As I taught our congregation to pray a financial hedge both for their personal finances and for our church finances, we began to break through! We learned to push the enemy away from our finances and to build a protective hedge around our surplus. Today, we are totally debt-free as a church. Our giving has continually increased, and our people are being tremendously blessed in the area of finances!

Here's how I pray a financial hedge: First, I thank the Lord for what I need - for the specific amount of money that I need. Then I bind the devil, and I command him to let go of what is mine. The Bible says that everything belongs to the Lord. He wants to bless us, so we have to ask, "Who's in the way?  Who is standing between God's blessing and me?" Satan! We bind him, and then we ask the Lord to send His angels to collect what belongs to us and bring it to us.

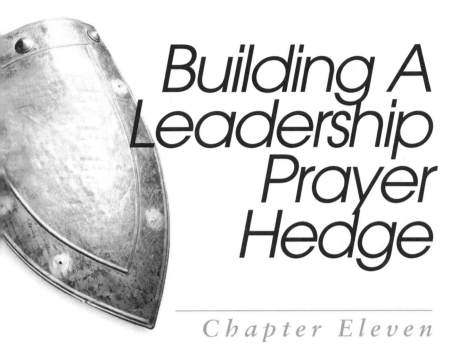

# Building A Leadership Prayer Hedge

*Chapter Eleven*

This hedge is especially applicable for pastors or others in ministry but could also apply to whatever work you do. The Bible instructs us to pray for those in leadership or in authority over us. One of the greatest needs leaders have is for a strong and consistent prayer covering. I believe we can never have enough people praying for us.

Leaders exercise influence and those who would influence others need much prayer. We must not only pray for our church leaders, but also for our leaders in government, education, business, the military, law enforcement, and for those in every other arena of influence.

Recently, the government of the Dominican Republic invited me to visit their nation. My agenda included a personal visit with President Hipolito Mejia. As President Mejia and I were conversing, I noticed an open Bible on his desk. I looked and to my delight, it was open to Psalm 91! When our meeting concluded, I asked the President about his Bible, and he shared with me that he finds great comfort in reading Psalm 91 everyday. Leaders desire prayer and God's protection!

Pastor Ken Wilde who operates the National Prayer Center in Washington D.C. regularly leads groups of intercessors on tours to Capitol Hill. As part of the Washington prayer experience, Pastor Ken takes these groups to visit their state and federal representatives. He and the intercessors offer to pray for their leaders. The eagerness of government officials to receive prayer has been a wonderful surprise to many. They readily welcome prayer and are truly thankful for it!

I have been amazed even in my own city of Utica, New York to see the response of government leaders as we have offered to pray for them. Our city went through a crisis in the mid-nineties. Businesses were closing or relocating and people were leaving the area in droves. During that season, our county had the highest population loss in America!

At that time, CBS 48 Hours interviewed our mayor. The program detailed the loss of business and the decay of our inner city. At one point, the city had to bring in the National Guard to demolish the multitude of houses that were abandoned and burnt out. The segment that aired nationally ended with the T.V. reporter asking our mayor, "What is your city's greatest need?" The mayor quickly responded, "We need a miracle!"

Mike Hughes, one of our staff pastors and our music minister, wrote a song together with his wife, Tammy, in response to the mayor's statement. The title of the song is *"Come To Our City."*

*"For too long, Lord, we've slept*
*while you mourned our city's pain.*
*Our hearts and our ears were closed,*
*While you heard the smallest child's cry.*
*But now we can feel the beat of*
*your heart and hear the call*
*To rise from our selfish world*
*and join our hands with yours*
*So Lord we pray -*

*Come to our city, Lord! We need a miracle!*
*This is our heart's cry. We can*
*no longer turn away*
*While others are suffering and*

*bound by their pain.*
*Come to our city, Lord.*
*Let blessings shower down*
*And rivers of mercy heal our land.*
*And in every heart and mind,*
*Lord, let your glory shine- give us a miracle.*

*We stood divided by walls of hostility*
*and pride, unwilling to reconcile, though your*
*heart's desire was that we be one.*
*But now we can see that there's more*
*to bind us than keep us apart.*
*Now burning as one bright flame,*
*we come in Jesus name,*
*And this is our prayer -*

*Come to our city, Lord! We need a miracle!*
*This is our heart's cry.*
*We can no longer stand alone,*
*For we are one body - the body of Christ.*

*So come to our city, Lord.*
*Send your revival fire!*
*We know that we cannot be denied,*
*When together we pray as one*
*and worship your only Son.*
*So give us a miracle.*"

Our church began to pray each hedge of protection around our city and its leaders. We petitioned God to begin to do miracles in our city. Many wonderful changes began to take place. Corruption began to be exposed and as it was confronted properly, the blessing of God began to be poured out. *Proverbs 11:11* states, *"The good influence of godly citizens causes a city to prosper, but the moral decay of the wicked drives it downhill"(TLB).*

In January of 2000, I was invited to give the invocation at the inauguration for our mayor and city council. Before I spoke, our choir sang for the assembled government leaders, "Come to our city, Lord! We need a miracle!" They loved it! I had the words of the song written in calligraphy and beautifully framed. We presented it as a gift to our city leaders.

A short time later, the mayor and city council presented us with an official proclamation honoring our church's leadership and influence in inspiring hope and faith during a very difficult season for our city. The proclamation also stated that the framed words of the song would hang forever in our city council chambers! In January 2004, the city again asked me to give the invocation for our mayor and city council and as I looked about, there on the wall still hung those words of faith.

## Ministries Need Greater Prayer Covering

I constantly pray for the church I pastor. I pray that everything we do and everything we are would represent the kingdom of God and bring honor and glory to the Lord. I pray that every word preached from our pulpit and all of our worship would bring only glory and honor to God and would not dishonor Him in any way.

We have had many, great meetings in our church. We have had good ministry, and we continue to host and receive honorable men and women of God into the church. We also pray a hedge of protection around the church body. We pray a hedge around every ministry of the church - our children, our teens, our singles, our home groups, our music ministry, our leadership, our ministry to the poor, etc. We pray for those involved in each specific ministry, that God would keep His hedge around them, and that the ministries would be effective and fruitful.

Furthermore, as our leaders go and minister in other churches, we pray a hedge of God's protection over them and those to whom they minister. We pray that the name of the Lord would be magnified in their activities and that God's kingdom would increase. We are determined to send and to receive people whose ministry advances the kingdom, and we pray a hedge of protection around the ministries to that end.

The warfare against those in ministry is both real and very intense. It is imperative that pastors have a prayer hedge built around them continually. I teach our people to pray each of the seven hedges around our pastors. For leaders to be effective and have long lasting, fruitful ministries, they must have a consistent prayer covering.

> **2 Corinthians 1:11** *"But you must help us too by praying for us. For much thanks and praise will go to God from you who see his wonderful answers to your prayers for our safety!"*(TLB).

## Praying For Leaders

1. Make a commitment to pray
   for them regularly and by name.
   Can you hear the Apostle Paul's cry
   for prayer covering? Every pastor
   senses the same need.

> **I Thessalonians 5:25** – *"Brethren pray for us."*
> **Romans 15:30** - *"Will you be my prayer partners? For the Lord Jesus Christ's sake and because of your love for me - given to you by the Holy Spirit - pray much with me for my work"* (TLB).

2. Pray that they would always walk
   in moral purity and integrity in all areas.

> **Hebrews 13:18** - *"Pray for us. We are sure that we have a clear conscience, because we always want to do the right thing"* (NCV).

3. Pray that God would supply all
   their needs and bless them with abundance.

> **Philippians 4:19** - *"And my God shall supply all your need according to His riches in glory by Christ Jesus."*

4. Pray that they would walk in health, and that the Lord would continually renew their strength.

*3 John 2* - *"Beloved, I pray that you may prosper in all things and be in health, just as your soul prospers."*

5. Pray that their marriages and families would be blessed, strengthened and protected.

*Psalm 128:1-6* - *"Blessings on all who reverence and trust the Lord - on all who obey Him! 2 Their reward shall be prosperity and happiness. 3 Your wife shall be contented in your home. And look at all those children! There they sit around the dinner table as vigorous and healthy as young olive trees. 4 That is God's reward to those who reverence and trust Him. 5 May the Lord continually bless you with heaven's blessings as well as with human joys. 6 May you live to enjoy your grandchildren! And may God bless Israel!"* (CEV).

6. Pray for wisdom, understanding and strategy in all situations. Pray for the ability to make wise choices and decisions.

*Ephesians 1:16-18* - *"So I never stop being grateful for you, as I mention you in my prayers. 17 I ask the glorious Father and God of our Lord Jesus Christ to give you His Spirit. The Spirit will make you wise and let you understand what it means to know God. 18 My prayer is that light will flood your hearts and that you will understand the hope that was given to you when God chose you. Then you will discover the glorious blessings that will be yours together with all of God's people"* (CEV).

7. Pray that they would become greater communicators of God's Word - that there would always be a fresh anointing of the Holy Spirit upon the proclamation of God's Word.

*Colossians 4:3-4* -*"Be sure to pray that God will make a way for us to spread his message and explain the mystery about Christ, even though I am in jail for doing this. 4 Please pray that I will make the message as clear as possible"*(CEV).

8. Pray that God would surround them with faithful people who will be a source of strength and encouragement.

*Exodus 17:1* - *"Later, when Moses' arms became tired, the men put a large rock under him and he sat on it. Then Aaron and Hur held up Moses' hands -Aaron on one side and Hur on the other. They kept his hands steady until the sun went down"* (NCV).

9. Pray that God will deliver them from satanic attacks, roadblocks and frustrations.

*2 Thessalonians 3:1-2* - *"And now, brothers and sisters, pray for us that the Lord's teaching will continue to spread quickly and that people will give honor to that teaching, just as happened with you.2 And pray that we will be protected from stubborn and evil people, because not all people believe"* (NCV).

## 10. Pray for greater open doors of ministry, increased influence and favor.

*I Corinthians 16:9* - *"For there is a wide-open door for a great work here, and many people are responding. But there are many who oppose me"* (NLT).

*Ephesians 6:19* - *"Also pray for me that when I speak, God will give me words so that I can tell the secret of the Good News without fear"* (NCV).

# Establishing God's Shield of Protection

*Chapter Twelve*

When I have prayed through these hedges of protection, I wrap up my prayer with *Isaiah 54:17* which says, *"No weapon formed against you will prosper, and you will refute every tongue that accuses you. This is the heritage of the servants of the Lord, and this is their vindication from me,' declares the Lord"*.

I confess God's Word that says no weapon forged against me will prevail, or as the *King James Version* of the Bible says, no weapon "will prosper." The word prosper or prevail means "to advance, rush forward, make progress, succeed, or prosper."

The Lord says that no weapon that is fashioned, designed, strategized, thought-out or launched against you will finish its course and reach you, if you'll pray. Something can start out to hurt or destroy you, but God says you can stop it from being completed. No weapon formed against you will come to its full end. It's not going to finish its course; it can be cut off.

For a long time, as I was praying this very scripture, I knew that there were weapons formed against us. I knew that there were arrows being fired against me in the spirit realm. The Lord would say to me, "Get up now and pray."

I would be in my prayer room, saying to those weapons, "I cast you down, in the name of Jesus." As I prayed, I could see arrows being launched and then falling to the ground. I would say to them, "You will not reach your target; you have hit a contrary wind," and they would fall powerless at my feet.

Every day, I declared that those arrows were falling powerless at my feet. I would say, "The Lord delivers me from secret traps. I will not fall under the power of any of those things. They're not going to reach my home; they're not going to reach our church. They fall powerless to the ground, and I refute every tongue that rises against us in judgment."

We must establish God's shield of protection around us in prayer. Our enemy is on the loose, but he is the defeated prince of an inferior kingdom. He knows that he cannot touch us, but he will not stop trying, so we pray. We wield the weapon of prayer against him as we ask the Lord to protect us in every way. My prayer for you is that you would indeed "live under the protection of God most high and stay in the shadow of God all-powerful."

# About the Author

Mike Servello is the senior pastor of Mt. Zion Ministries in Utica, New York, a church he has pastored for more than twenty years.

Mike serves on the Apostolic Leadership Team of Ministers Fellowship International.

He is also the founder and CEO of Compassion Coalition, a ministry which feeds tens of thousands of people annually in the U.S. and around the world.

Mike and his wife, Barbara, have been married for 30 years and have three adult children, Mike Jr., Joseph and Rachel.